TELL US WHAT YOU THINK

☆☆☆☆☆

Attach a photo *of your finished designs in your review!*

USA Store

Explore our ***HUGE*** *range!*

UK Store

CLAM COLORING
2023

The Fool

The Fool is a highly symbolic card in the Tarot deck, representing new beginnings, innocence, and spontaneity. The card depicts a young man standing on the edge of a cliff, with a small dog at his heels. The image is one of potential and adventure.

The Fool card suggests that you may be at the beginning of a new journey or adventure in your life. It can indicate that you are taking a leap of faith, stepping into the unknown, and trusting in the universe to guide you. This card can also suggest that you may need to let go of old patterns of thinking and behavior in order to embrace new opportunities.

The Fool is a reminder to approach life with a sense of openness and curiosity. It encourages us to embrace our inner child, to take risks, and to follow our intuition. This card can also indicate a need to be more spontaneous and to live in the moment, rather than worrying about the future.

The Fool can also be a symbol of rebirth and transformation. It suggests that by letting go of the past and embracing new beginnings, we can achieve a greater sense of freedom and authenticity. This card invites us to step outside of our comfort zones and to embrace the unknown, trusting that the universe will guide us on our journey.

Overall, the Fool is a card of new beginnings, potential, and adventure. It reminds us to approach life with a sense of openness and curiosity, and to embrace the unknown. The Fool is a powerful symbol of transformation and growth, as it encourages us to let go of the past and to trust in the process of life.

0
THE FOOL

Temperance

The Temperance card in the Tarot deck is a symbol of balance, harmony, and moderation. It represents the need to find a middle ground and to integrate opposing forces. The card depicts an angel with one foot in the water and the other on the land, pouring water from one cup to another. The image is one of equilibrium and flow.

The Temperance card suggests that you may be in a situation where you need to find balance and moderation. It can indicate that you are seeking harmony in your life, and that you may need to integrate different aspects of yourself in order to find it. This card can also suggest that you are in the process of healing, and that you need to take a gentle and compassionate approach to yourself and others.

The Temperance card is a reminder to approach life with a sense of calmness and patience. It suggests that by finding balance and moderation, you can achieve greater success and happiness. This card can also indicate a need to be flexible and adaptable, as life is constantly changing and evolving.

The Temperance card can also be a symbol of alchemy and transformation. It invites you to embrace the process of change and to trust in the unfolding of life. This card suggests that by integrating different aspects of yourself and finding a sense of harmony and flow, you can achieve a greater sense of wholeness and inner peace.

Overall, the Temperance card is a symbol of balance and harmony. It reminds us to approach life with a sense of calmness and patience, and to find a middle ground between opposing forces. The Temperance card is a powerful symbol of transformation and growth, as it encourages us to embrace change and to trust in the process of life.

XIV
TEMPERANCE

The Hanged Man

The Hanged Man is a profound and contemplative card in the Tarot deck. It represents sacrifice, surrender, and letting go. The card depicts a figure suspended upside down from a tree, with one foot tied to the trunk and the other crossed over the knee. The image is one of suspension and surrender.

The Hanged Man suggests that you may be in a situation where you need to let go of control and surrender to a greater power. This card can indicate that you are at a crossroads and that you need to pause and reflect on your situation before making a decision. It can also suggest that you may need to sacrifice something in order to move forward.

The Hanged Man is a reminder that sometimes, in order to achieve our goals, we need to let go of old beliefs and patterns of behavior. It can be a symbol of transformation and spiritual growth, as it invites us to see things from a different perspective and to question our assumptions. This card suggests that by surrendering to the flow of life and letting go of our attachments, we can find a greater sense of peace and harmony.

The Hanged Man can also indicate a willingness to endure hardship for a greater cause or purpose. It suggests that sometimes, we need to suffer in order to achieve a greater good. This card can be a reminder to stay true to your values and to have faith in the ultimate outcome, even if the path is difficult.

Overall, the Hanged Man is a card of sacrifice and surrender. It invites us to let go of our attachments and to trust in the unknown. It can be a symbol of transformation and growth, as it encourages us to question our assumptions and to see things from a different perspective. The Hanged Man reminds us that sometimes, in order to move forward, we need to let go and trust in the process.

XII
THE HANGED MAN

The Devil

The Devil is a powerful and often unsettling card in the Tarot deck. It represents temptation, addiction, and bondage. The card depicts a horned devil figure with a man and woman chained to a pedestal in front of him. The image is one of enslavement and domination.

The Devil card suggests that you may be caught up in patterns of behavior or addictions that are holding you back. It can indicate that you are trapped in a situation that feels impossible to escape from. This card is a warning that you may be giving into your fears and desires, even if they are harmful to you or others.

The Devil is a reminder that you have the power to break free from these negative patterns and to take control of your life. This card can be a call to action, urging you to confront your shadow self and to overcome your inner demons. It can also suggest that there may be external forces at play, such as toxic relationships or societal pressures, that are contributing to your sense of bondage.

The Devil card can be a symbol of transformation and liberation. It invites you to confront your fears and to embrace your true nature. This card suggests that by facing your fears and taking control of your life, you can break free from the chains that bind you and achieve a greater sense of freedom and fulfillment.

Overall, the Devil is a powerful and challenging card that asks us to confront our deepest fears and desires. It is a reminder that we have the power to break free from negative patterns and to live a life of greater meaning and purpose.

XV
THE DEVIL

The Moon

The Moon is a complex and mysterious card in the Tarot deck. It represents the unconscious mind, intuition, and the unknown. The card depicts a full moon in the night sky, with two dogs howling at the moon, and a crustacean emerging from a pool of water. The image is one of mystery and darkness.

The Moon card is often associated with fear, uncertainty, and confusion. It suggests that things may not be as they appear, and that there may be hidden aspects of a situation that need to be uncovered. This card can also indicate that your emotions are running high and that you may be experiencing mood swings or irrational thoughts.

The Moon is a reminder to trust your intuition and to listen to your inner voice. It may be necessary to explore your subconscious mind and to confront your fears in order to move forward. This card can also indicate that there are secrets or hidden motives at play, and that it's important to be aware of them.

The Moon can be a powerful symbol of transformation and spiritual growth. It invites you to embrace the unknown and to explore the depths of your psyche. The card suggests that there is a need to confront your shadow self and to integrate all aspects of your being. The Moon reminds us that even in the darkness, there is the potential for growth and enlightenment.

Overall, the Moon is a complex and powerful card that invites us to embrace the mysteries of life and to trust in our inner wisdom. It encourages us to face our fears and to explore the depths of our psyche, ultimately leading us to greater self-awareness and spiritual growth.

XVIII
THE MOON

The Tower

The Tower is one of the most striking and ominous cards in the Tarot deck. In most depictions of the card, a tower is depicted on fire, with people leaping from the windows to escape the flames. The image is one of chaos, destruction, and upheaval.

The Tower card represents sudden and unexpected change that can be both positive and negative. It can be a wake-up call or a crisis that forces you to abandon old ways of thinking and behaving. This card can indicate a major shift in your life, such as the loss of a job or the end of a relationship, or it could represent a major breakthrough or epiphany.

The Tower is a reminder that change is inevitable and that sometimes, it takes a dramatic event to shake us out of our complacency. The Tower can be a symbol of liberation, as it can free you from outdated beliefs, patterns, and structures that no longer serve your best interests.

At its core, the Tower card is about letting go of what no longer serves you and being open to new possibilities. It may be a painful process, but it's necessary for growth and transformation. The Tower reminds us that even in the darkest moments, there is the potential for renewal and rebirth.

XVI
THE TOWER

Death

The Death card in the Tarot deck is one of the most misunderstood cards, as it often evokes fear and anxiety. However, this card is not a symbol of physical death, but rather a powerful symbol of transformation, rebirth, and letting go. The card depicts a skeleton riding a white horse, holding a black flag with a white rose on it. The image is one of profound change and release.

The Death card suggests that you may be in a period of profound transformation and change. It can indicate that old patterns, beliefs, or relationships are coming to an end, and that you need to let go of them in order to move forward. This card can also suggest that you may be experiencing a significant loss or change, but that this change is necessary for your growth and evolution.

The Death card is a reminder that death is a natural part of the cycle of life, and that sometimes we need to let go of old things in order to make way for the new. It can be a symbol of liberation and freedom, as it invites us to release ourselves from the past and to embrace the unknown.

The Death card can also be a symbol of spiritual transformation and rebirth. It suggests that by letting go of our attachments and embracing change, we can achieve a greater sense of inner peace and harmony. This card invites us to trust in the process of life, and to have faith that new beginnings will arise from the ashes of the old.

Overall, the Death card is a symbol of profound change, transformation, and letting go. It reminds us that sometimes we need to release old patterns, beliefs, or relationships in order to move forward. The Death card is a powerful symbol of spiritual growth and evolution, as it encourages us to embrace the unknown and to trust in the process of life.

XIII
DEATH

The Hermit

The Hermit is a highly symbolic card in the Tarot deck, representing introspection, solitude, and spiritual enlightenment. The card depicts an old man holding a lantern, standing alone on top of a mountain. The image is one of solitude and inner wisdom.

The Hermit card suggests that you may be in a period of introspection and reflection. It can indicate that you need to take some time alone to reflect on your life and your spiritual path. This card can also suggest that you may be seeking greater clarity and understanding, and that you need to look within yourself to find it.

The Hermit is a reminder that sometimes we need to withdraw from the world in order to gain greater insight and understanding. It encourages us to take time for meditation, contemplation, and self-reflection. This card can also indicate a need to seek out a spiritual teacher or mentor who can guide us on our path.

The Hermit can also be a symbol of enlightenment and spiritual awakening. It suggests that by going within ourselves and connecting with our inner wisdom, we can achieve a greater sense of inner peace and harmony. This card invites us to embrace our spiritual journey and to trust in the guidance of the universe.

Overall, the Hermit is a card of introspection, solitude, and spiritual enlightenment. It reminds us to take time for self-reflection and to seek out guidance on our spiritual path. The Hermit is a powerful symbol of inner wisdom and guidance, as it encourages us to look within ourselves to find the answers we seek.

IX
THE HERMIT

Strength

The Strength card in the Tarot deck is a symbol of courage, inner strength, and perseverance. The card depicts a woman with a lion, holding the lion's jaws open. The image is one of physical and emotional strength.

The Strength card suggests that you have the inner strength and courage to overcome any challenges you may be facing. It can indicate that you need to tap into your inner reserves of strength and resilience in order to overcome obstacles and achieve your goals. This card can also suggest that you need to be patient and persistent in order to succeed.

The Strength card is a reminder that true strength comes from within. It encourages us to cultivate our inner strength and resilience, and to have faith in our ability to overcome any difficulties that come our way. This card can also be a symbol of compassion, as it suggests that true strength comes from a place of love and kindness.

The Strength card can also be a symbol of the power of the mind over the body. It suggests that by harnessing the power of our thoughts and beliefs, we can achieve great things. This card invites us to trust in our intuition and inner wisdom, and to have faith in our ability to create positive change in our lives.

Overall, the Strength card is a symbol of courage, resilience, and inner strength. It reminds us that true strength comes from within, and that we have the power to overcome any challenges we may face. The Strength card is a powerful symbol of the human spirit, as it encourages us to tap into our inner reserves of strength and to have faith in our ability to create positive change in our lives.

VIII
STRENGTH

Wheel of Fortune

The Wheel of Fortune is a powerful and dynamic card in the Tarot deck, representing cycles of change, fate, and destiny. The card depicts a large wheel with different symbols on it, including the four elements, the zodiac, and the Hebrew letters.

The Wheel of Fortune card suggests that life is constantly changing, and that we must learn to adapt to these changes in order to achieve our goals. It can indicate that we are in a period of transition, and that we need to be flexible and open-minded in order to make the most of the opportunities that come our way.

The Wheel of Fortune is also a symbol of fate and destiny. It suggests that our lives are not entirely within our control, and that we must accept the twists and turns of our path with grace and resilience. This card can also be a reminder that everything in life is cyclical, and that what goes around comes around.

The Wheel of Fortune is a powerful symbol of the power of the universe. It suggests that there is a higher power at work in our lives, and that we must trust in this power to guide us on our path. This card invites us to let go of our need for control, and to have faith in the unfolding of our lives.

Overall, the Wheel of Fortune is a symbol of cycles of change, fate, and destiny. It reminds us that life is constantly in motion, and that we must learn to adapt to these changes in order to succeed. The Wheel of Fortune is a powerful reminder that there is a higher power at work in our lives, and that we must trust in this power to guide us on our path.

X
WHEEL OF FORTUNE

The Star

The Star card in the Tarot deck is a symbol of hope, inspiration, and renewal. The card depicts a woman pouring water from two jugs, with eight stars shining brightly in the sky above her. The image is one of beauty, tranquility, and peace.

The Star card suggests that you are entering a period of renewal and healing. It can indicate that you have been through a difficult time, but that you are now ready to move forward with renewed optimism and hope. This card invites you to connect with your inner self, and to tap into your intuition and creativity in order to achieve your goals.

The Star card is also a symbol of inspiration and guidance. It suggests that you are being guided by a higher power, and that you should trust in your intuition and inner wisdom. This card can indicate that you are on the right path, and that you should have faith in your ability to achieve your dreams.

The Star card is a reminder that hope and inspiration are always available to us, no matter how difficult our circumstances may be. This card invites us to find the beauty in life, and to appreciate the simple pleasures that bring us joy. It can also be a symbol of community, as it suggests that we are all connected, and that we should support and inspire each other in our journeys.

Overall, the Star card is a symbol of hope, inspiration, and renewal. It reminds us that we are not alone, and that we have the power to tap into our inner resources in order to achieve our goals. The Star card is a powerful reminder to trust in ourselves and in the universe, and to have faith in our ability to create positive change in our lives.

XVII
THE STAR

Judgement

The Judgment card in the Tarot deck is a symbol of rebirth, awakening, and judgment. The card depicts an angel blowing a trumpet, with people rising from their graves and looking up at the angel in awe. The image is one of spiritual awakening, transformation, and judgment.

The Judgment card suggests that you are going through a process of rebirth and transformation. It can indicate that you have reached a turning point in your life, and that you are now ready to let go of the past and move forward with a renewed sense of purpose and clarity. This card invites you to embrace your true self and to let go of anything that is holding you back.

The Judgment card is also a symbol of judgment and accountability. It suggests that you will be held accountable for your actions, and that you should take responsibility for the choices that you have made. This card can indicate that you will be judged by others, but it also reminds you that you have the power to judge yourself and to make amends for any mistakes that you have made.

The Judgment card is a powerful symbol of spiritual awakening and transformation. It suggests that you are being called to a higher purpose, and that you should embrace your spiritual path with enthusiasm and dedication. This card can also be a symbol of forgiveness and redemption, as it suggests that you have the power to forgive yourself and others, and to move forward with a sense of peace and healing.

Overall, the Judgment card is a symbol of rebirth, awakening, and judgment. It reminds us that we have the power to transform our lives and to create positive change in the world. The Judgment card is a powerful reminder to embrace our true selves, to take responsibility for our actions, and to let go of the past in order to create a brighter future.

XX
JUDGEMENT

Justice

The Justice card in the Tarot deck is a symbol of fairness, balance, and truth. The card depicts a woman sitting on a throne, holding a sword and scales. The image is one of authority, integrity, and judgment.

The Justice card suggests that you are seeking balance and fairness in your life. It can indicate that you are going through a period of evaluation and decision-making, and that you are looking for clarity and truth in your choices. This card invites you to be honest with yourself and to take responsibility for your actions.

The Justice card is also a symbol of karma and consequences. It suggests that you will be held accountable for your actions, and that you should consider the impact of your choices on others. This card can indicate that you may need to make amends for past mistakes in order to create a sense of balance and harmony in your life.

The Justice card is a powerful symbol of integrity and authority. It suggests that you have the power to make fair and just decisions, and that you should act with integrity in all aspects of your life. This card can also be a symbol of legal matters, as it suggests that you may be involved in a legal case or dispute.

Overall, the Justice card is a symbol of fairness, balance, and truth. It reminds us that we have the power to make just and ethical decisions, and that we should act with integrity in all aspects of our lives. The Justice card is a powerful reminder to seek balance and fairness, and to take responsibility for our actions in order to create a more just and harmonious world.

XI
JUSTICE

The World

The World card in the Tarot deck is a symbol of completion, fulfillment, and unity. The card depicts a naked woman surrounded by a wreath, with four figures in each corner representing the four elements of earth, air, fire, and water. The image is one of wholeness, harmony, and interconnectedness.

The World card suggests that you have reached a point of completion in your journey. It can indicate that you have achieved a sense of fulfillment and satisfaction, and that you are ready to move on to the next phase of your life. This card invites you to celebrate your accomplishments and to feel a sense of pride and gratitude for all that you have achieved.

The World card is also a symbol of unity and interconnectedness. It suggests that you are connected to all things, and that you have a sense of oneness with the universe. This card can indicate that you are experiencing a deep sense of harmony and balance in your life, and that you are living in alignment with your true purpose and values.

The World card is a powerful symbol of completion and wholeness. It suggests that you have integrated all aspects of yourself, and that you have achieved a sense of inner peace and harmony. This card can also be a symbol of travel and adventure, as it suggests that you may be embarking on a journey or experiencing a sense of expansion and growth.

Overall, the World card is a symbol of completion, fulfillment, and unity. It reminds us that we are all interconnected, and that we have the power to create a harmonious and fulfilling life. The World card is a powerful reminder to celebrate our accomplishments, to feel a sense of gratitude and oneness with the universe, and to continue on our journey of growth and self-discovery.

XXI
THE WORLD

The Sun card in the Tarot deck is a symbol of positivity, vitality, and success. The card depicts a child riding a white horse under a bright sun, surrounded by sunflowers. The image is one of joy, optimism, and vitality.

The Sun card suggests that you are experiencing a sense of joy and vitality in your life. It can indicate that you are feeling confident, successful, and full of energy. This card invites you to embrace your sense of positivity and to share your light with others. It encourages you to be open and honest in your communications, and to be true to yourself.

The Sun card is also a symbol of new beginnings and growth. It suggests that you are on the path to success and that you are moving forward with confidence and enthusiasm. This card invites you to embrace your sense of optimism and to have faith in the future.

The Sun card can also indicate that you are experiencing a sense of inner peace and contentment. It suggests that you are living in alignment with your true purpose and values, and that you are connected to your inner wisdom and intuition.

Overall, the Sun card is a symbol of positivity, vitality, and success. It reminds us to embrace our sense of joy and optimism, to have faith in the future, and to share our light with others. The Sun card is a powerful reminder to stay true to ourselves and to live in alignment with our true purpose and values.

XIX
THE SUN

The Magician

The Magician tarot card is the first card in the Major Arcana of the Tarot deck. It represents manifestation, creativity, and transformation. The card features a figure, often depicted as a young man, standing behind a table with various objects, including a wand, cup, sword, and pentacle.

The Magician is a symbol of power and mastery. The card suggests that you have the ability to manifest your desires and achieve your goals through your creativity and resourcefulness. It invites you to tap into your inner power and harness your abilities to create positive change in your life.

The Magician also represents the power of communication and the ability to influence others. It suggests that you have the power to express yourself clearly and persuasively, and to use your words and actions to create positive outcomes in your life.

The Magician card can also indicate that you are at a crossroads in your life, with the potential for new opportunities and transformation. It invites you to trust your instincts and take action to create the future you desire.

Overall, the Magician tarot card is a powerful symbol of manifestation, creativity, and transformation. It reminds us to tap into our inner power and use our abilities to create positive change in our lives. The Magician card is a powerful reminder to trust in ourselves, take action, and embrace the opportunities for growth and transformation that are available to us.

I
THE MAGICIAN

The High Priestess

The High Priestess tarot card is a powerful symbol of intuition, wisdom, and mystery. It is the second card in the Major Arcana of the Tarot deck and features a woman sitting on a throne between two pillars, with a veil behind her.

The High Priestess represents the power of intuition and inner wisdom. She invites us to trust our instincts and listen to our inner voice, as it holds the key to our deepest truths and desires. She represents the feminine energy of receptivity and introspection, and reminds us to be still and listen to the whispers of our soul.

The High Priestess is also a symbol of mystery and hidden knowledge. She suggests that there are secrets and mysteries waiting to be uncovered, and that we must be patient and open to receive them. She represents the power of the unknown and the unseen, and reminds us to have faith in the universe and the greater wisdom that surrounds us.

The High Priestess card can also indicate a need for solitude and reflection. It suggests that we may benefit from taking time for introspection and self-examination, to gain clarity and perspective on our lives and our path forward.

Overall, the High Priestess tarot card is a powerful symbol of intuition, wisdom, and mystery. She reminds us to trust our inner voice, be open to the unknown, and embrace the power of introspection and reflection. The High Priestess card is a powerful reminder to be patient, have faith, and trust in the greater wisdom of the universe.

II
THE HIGH PRIESTESS

TELL US WHAT YOU THINK

SCAN ME!

☆☆☆☆☆

***Attach a photo** of your finished designs in your review!*

USA Store

*Explore our **HUGE** range!*

UK Store

CLAM COLORING
2023

© Copyright SSJH GROUP Ltd 2023 - All rights reserved.

The content contained within this book may not be reproduced, duplicated or transmitted without direct written permission from the author or the publisher.

Under no circumstances will any blame or legal responsibility be held against the publisher, or author, for any damages, reparation, or monetary loss due to the information contained within this book. Either directly or indirectly. You are responsible for your own choices, actions, and results.

Legal Notice:

This book is copyright protected. This book is only for personal use. You cannot amend, distribute, sell, use, quote or paraphrase any part, or the content within this book, without the consent of the author or publisher.

Disclaimer Notice:

Please note the information contained within this document is for entertainment purposes only. No warranties of any kind are declared or implied. Readers acknowledge that the author is not engaging in the rendering of legal, financial, medical or professional advice. The content within this book has been derived from various sources. Please consult a licensed professional before attempting any techniques outlined in this book.

By reading this document, the reader agrees that under no circumstances is the author responsible for any losses, direct or indirect, which are incurred as a result of the use of the information contained within this document, including, but not limited to, — errors, omissions, or inaccuracies.

Printed in Great Britain
by Amazon